DJIBOUTI 2016 HUMAN RIGHTS REPORT

EXECUTIVE SUMMARY

Djibouti is a republic with a strong elected president and a weak legislature. In 2010 parliament amended the constitution to remove term limits, facilitating the 2011 and 2016 re-election of President Ismail Omar Guelleh for a third and fourth term. Three independent and two opposition candidates also participated in the April presidential election. International observers from the African Union, the Intergovernmental Authority on Development, and the Arab League characterized the election as "peaceful," "calm," and "sufficiently free and transparent," but noted irregularities. Most opposition groups did not characterize the elections as free and fair. Opposition parties participated in February 2013 legislative elections for the first time in 10 years; perceived flaws in the vote fueled months of protest and an opposition boycott of the National Assembly until the signing of a framework agreement with the government in 2014. International observers from the African Union, the Intergovernmental Authority on Development, the Organization of Islamic Cooperation, and the Arab League had characterized the 2013 elections as free and fair, an assessment disputed both domestically and by some other international observers.

Civilian authorities maintained effective control over security forces.

The most serious human rights problems included: the government's abridgement of the ability of citizens to choose or significantly influence their government by suppressing the opposition and refusing to allow several opposition groups to form legally recognized political parties; harassing, abusing, and detaining government critics; denying the population access to independent sources of information; and restricting freedoms of speech and assembly.

Other human rights problems included the use of excessive force, including torture, harsh prison conditions, arbitrary arrest and prolonged pretrial detention, denial of fair public trial, interference with privacy rights, restrictions on freedoms of association and religion, lack of protection for refugees, corruption, discrimination and violence against women, female genital mutilation/cutting (FGM/C), child abuse, trafficking in persons, discrimination against persons with disabilities, and discrimination against persons with HIV/AIDS and the lesbian, gay, bisexual, transgender, and intersex (LGBTI) community. The government restricted worker rights, and child labor, including forced child labor, occurred.

Impunity was a problem. The government seldom took steps to prosecute or punish officials who committed abuses, whether in the security services or elsewhere in the government.

Section 1. Respect for the Integrity of the Person, Including Freedom from:

a. Arbitrary Deprivation of Life and other Unlawful or Politically Motivated Killings

There were reports the government or its agents committed arbitrary or unlawful killings. According to political opposition members and domestic human rights organizations, security force use of excessive force resulted in deaths.

According to human rights groups, on February 28, authorities in Tadjourah detained and fatally beat two individuals, Houmed Ismail and Abdo Ahmed Momin.

In December 2015 the government investigated law enforcement officials and civilians allegedly responsible for killing as many as 30 persons gathering for a religious ceremony the same month. The government did not find any law enforcement officials responsible for the deaths; several civilian cases related to the same incident remained pending.

Authorities seldom took known actions to investigate reported cases of arbitrary or unlawful killings from previous years or to punish suspected perpetrators.

Authorities reportedly investigated the 2012 death of Hafez Mohamed and closed the case during the year. Authorities stated a gendarme's tear gas canister punctured Mohamed's liver. The state prosecutor concluded the death was an accident, and the government reportedly paid an indemnity to Hafez's family.

b. Disappearance

There were no reports of politically motivated disappearances.

c. Torture and Other Cruel, Inhuman, or Degrading Treatment or Punishment

The constitution and law prohibit such practices; however, there were reports security forces beat and tortured detainees.

Security forces arrested and abused journalists, demonstrators, and opposition members.

On January 14, authorities in Balbala reportedly arrested president of the Opposition Youth Movement Zakaria Rirache Miguil during a meeting of opposition youth in his home. According to opposition and human rights groups, security officials beat and tortured Miguil, who allegedly held a 24-hour hunger strike to protest prison conditions. Security officials reportedly arrested Miguil on suspicion of preparing a protest among youth against President Guelleh's candidacy for a fourth mandate. Authorities released him after one week for lack of evidence.

According to opposition members, security forces arrested, beat, and shot several opposition leaders allegedly linked to the December 2015 incident. Government officials stated they investigated the case, but there was no evidence corroborating the allegations.

Prison and Detention Center Conditions

International organizations reported prison conditions remained harsh. The country had one central prison, Gabode, in the capital and a second, smaller regional prison in Obock, as well as small jails supervised by local police or gendarmes. These jails often served as holding cells before detainees were moved to the central prison. Nagad Detention Facility, operated by police, primarily held irregular migrants and was not part of the prison system. There were reports police and gendarmes abused prisoners.

Physical Conditions: Gabode Prison had a maximum intended capacity of 350 inmates but often held more than 600, approximately 30 of whom were women. Conditions of detention for women were similar to those of men, although less crowded. There were generally fewer than 30 juvenile prisoners. Authorities allowed young children of female prisoners to stay with their mothers. Due to space constraints, authorities did not always hold pretrial detainees separately from convicted prisoners, nor were violent offenders always separated from nonviolent offenders. Authorities separated opposition supporters from the rest of the prison population and reportedly provided them with worse conditions than other prisoners for their incarceration. Authorities also reportedly provided poor lighting and heating, limited potable water and ventilation, and inhumane sanitation options for the prison population.

Prisoners with mental disabilities, who constituted a growing percentage of the prison population, did not receive adequate care. They were kept in the infirmary, although separately from seriously ill prisoners.

Conditions in jails, which held detainees until their summary release or transfer to the central prison, were poor. Jails had no formal system to feed or segregate prisoners and did not provide medical services. Prisoners were fed, but not on a regular basis.

Conditions at Nagad Detention Facility were poor, although detainees had access to potable water, food, and medical treatment. Authorities deported most detainees within 24 hours of arrest. While normally used for irregular migrants and prisoners of war, the government used Nagad Detention Facility in previous years as a temporary holding place for civilians arrested during political demonstrations. There were no such reports during the year, however.

No statistics were available on the number of overall prisoner and detainee deaths.

Administration: There was no prison ombudsman, but prisoners and detainees could submit complaints, showing evident censorship, through prison authorities to judicial officials to request investigation of inhumane conditions, which officials carried out in cases they deemed credible.

Independent Monitoring: The government granted prison access to foreign embassies and the International Committee of the Red Cross (ICRC) only for cases of foreign citizens detained in the prisons. The government refused access to foreign embassies to monitor the prisons. Authorities allowed ICRC regional representatives based in Nairobi to visit Nagad Detention Facility and Gabode Prison quarterly and to conduct visits to individual detainees.

d. Arbitrary Arrest or Detention

The law prohibits arbitrary arrest and detention, but the government did not respect these prohibitions.

Role of the Police and Security Apparatus

Security forces include the National Police under the Ministry of Interior, the army and National Gendarmerie under the Ministry of Defense, and the Coast Guard under the Ministry of Transport. An elite Republican Guard unit protects the president and reports directly to the presidency. A separate National Security Service also reports directly to the presidency. The National Police are responsible for security within Djibouti City and have primary control over immigration and customs procedures for all land border-crossing points. The National Gendarmerie is responsible for all security outside of Djibouti City and has the responsibility of protecting critical infrastructure within the city, such as at the international airport. The army is responsible for defense of the national borders. The Coast Guard enforces maritime laws, including interdicting pirates, smugglers, traffickers, and irregular migrants.

Security forces were generally effective, although corruption was a problem in all services, particularly in the lower ranks where wages were low. Each security force has a unit responsible for investigating allegations of misconduct, and the Ministry of Justice is responsible for prosecution. No known formal complaints of misconduct were filed during the year. Authorities took no known action to investigate complaints of misconduct from previous years. Impunity was a serious problem.

The National Police has a Human Rights Office and has integrated human rights education into the police academy curriculum.

Arrest Procedures and Treatment of Detainees

The law requires arrest warrants and stipulates the government may not detain a person beyond 48 hours without an examining magistrate's formal charge; however, the government generally did not respect the law, especially in rural areas. Authorities may hold detainees another 48 hours with the prior approval of the public prosecutor. The law provides that law enforcement should promptly notify detainees of the charges against them, although there were delays. The law requires that all persons, including those charged with political or national security offenses, be tried within eight months of arraignment, although the government did not respect this right. The law contains provisions for bail, but authorities rarely made use of it. Detainees have the right to prompt access to an attorney of their choice, which generally occurred, although there were exceptions. In criminal cases, the state provides attorneys for detainees who cannot afford legal representation. In instances of unlawful detention, detainees could get court ordered release but not compensation.

Arbitrary Arrest: During the year government officials arbitrarily arrested journalists, opposition members, academics, and demonstrators, often without warrants.

For example, on August 9, authorities arrested journalist Kadar Abdi Ibrahim at the Ambouli airport for allegedly attempting to record airport officials preventing opposition figure Hamoud Abdi Soultan from leaving Djibouti. Opposition members reported officials confiscated Kadar's iPad, deleted all of his pictures, and detained him for three days. They also stated authorities prevented him from seeing a lawyer or his family and from eating and drinking water. He was subsequently released without charge.

Pretrial Detention: Lengthy pretrial detention was a problem, and approximately 20 percent of the prison population was in pretrial detention. Prisoners often waited two, three, or more years for their trials to begin. Judicial inefficiency and a lack of experienced legal staff contributed to the problem.

Security officials held Abdourahman Mohamed Guelleh in pretrial detention from December 2015 until April 5 based on allegations of encouraging violent protests in connection with the December 21 incident. His case was still pending, but he was released on probation.

e. Denial of Fair Public Trial

The constitution and law provide for an independent judiciary, but the judiciary lacked independence and was inefficient. There were reports of judicial corruption. Authorities often did not respect constitutional provisions for a fair trial.

Trial Procedures

The legal system is based on legislation and executive decrees, French codified law adopted at independence, Islamic law (sharia), and nomadic traditions.

The law states the accused is innocent until proven guilty, but trials did not proceed in accordance with the presumption of innocence. Trials generally were public. A presiding judge and two associate judges hear cases. Three lay assessors, who are not members of the bench but are considered sufficiently knowledgeable to comprehend court proceedings, assist the presiding judge. The government chooses lay assessors from the public. In criminal cases the court consists of the presiding judge of the court of appeal, two lay assessors, and four jurors selected from voter registration lists. The law provides that detainees be notified promptly and in detail of the charges against them. Although the law requires the state to provide detainees with free interpretation when needed, such services were not always made available. Detainees have the right to prompt access to an attorney of their choice. Defendants have the right to be present, consult with an attorney in a timely manner, confront witnesses, present witnesses and evidence on their own behalf, and generally have adequate time and facilities to prepare a defense. They have the right to access government-held evidence. Authorities generally respected these rights. The indigent have a right to legal counsel in criminal and civil matters but sometimes did not have legal representation. Defendants have the right not to be compelled to testify or confess guilt. Defendants have the right of appeal, although the appeals process was lengthy. The law extends these rights to all citizens.

Traditional law often applied in cases involving conflict resolution and victim compensation. Traditional law stipulates that a price be paid to the victim's family for crimes such as murder and rape. Most parties preferred traditional court rulings for sensitive issues such as rape, where a peaceful consensus among those involved was valued over the rights of victims. Families often pressured victims to abide by traditional court rulings.

Political Prisoners and Detainees

There were arbitrary arrests of opposition supporters. On January 1, gendarmes arrested a prominent opposition leader for 24 hours.

Civil Judicial Procedures and Remedies

In cases of human rights violations, citizens could address correspondence to the National Human Rights Commission. On a variety of matters, citizens could also seek assistance from the Ombudsman's Office, which often helped resolve administrative disputes between government branches. Citizens could also appeal decisions to the African Court on Human and Peoples' Rights. The government did not always comply with those bodies' decisions and recommendations pertaining to human rights.

f. Arbitrary or Unlawful Interference with Privacy, Family, Home, or Correspondence

Although the constitution and law prohibit such actions, the government did not respect these prohibitions. The law requires authorities to obtain a warrant before conducting searches on private property, but the government did not always respect the law. Government critics claimed the government monitored their communications and kept their homes under surveillance.

The government monitored digital communications intended to be private and punished their authors (see section 2.a., Internet Freedom).

While membership in a political party was not required for government jobs, civil servants who publicly criticized the government faced reprisals at work, including suspension, dismissal, and nonpayment of salaries.

Section 2. Respect for Civil Liberties, Including:

a. Freedom of Speech and Press

The constitution and law allow for freedom of speech and press, provided the exercise of these freedoms complies with the law and respects "the honor of others." The government did not respect these rights. The law provides prison sentences for media offenses.

<u>Freedom of Speech and Expression</u>: Individuals who criticized the government publicly or privately could face reprisals. Plainclothes security agents in mosques monitored the content of sermons during Friday prayers.

On January 14, authorities arrested Kadar Abdi Ibrahim, university professor and journalist and publisher of biweekly opposition magazine *l'Aurore*, after he published a picture of a child killed during the December 2015 incident. Ibrahim spent one night in custody and was then released. On January 19, a judge suspended Ibrahim's magazine for two months and gave him a suspended two-month jail sentence. In February 2015 Ibrahim was fired by presidential decree from his position at the university for expressing political beliefs in the workplace.

Another opposition member and two persons linked to the December 2015 incident were also fired by presidential decree from their government positions.

<u>Press and Media Freedoms</u>: There were no privately owned or independent newspapers in the country. Printing facilities for mass media were government

owned, which created obstacles for those wishing to publish criticism of the government. The principal newspaper, *La Nation*, maintained a monopoly on domestic news.

On April 2, the government expelled BBC journalists, including BBC's Africa security correspondent, from the country. According to government officials, the BBC journalists did not have proper media accreditation to report on the presidential election scheduled for April 8. The BBC asserted they did have official media accreditation and interviewed the foreign minister and an opposition candidate on April 1, after which authorities detained the journalists and deported them the next morning.

Opposition political groups and civil society activists circulated newsletters and other materials that criticized the government via e-mail and social media sites. President of the Djiboutian Human Rights League (LDDH) Omar Ali Ewado published a list of persons who allegedly died in the December 2015 incident; the number of names exceeded the government's official death toll. Government officials stated Ewado fabricated the names and death toll. Authorities charged Ewado with defamation, and he spent 45 days in pretrial detention. On February 14, authorities granted Ewado probation. On April 30, the Supreme Court dropped all charges against him.

The government owned the only radio and television stations, operated by Radio Television Djibouti. The official media generally did not criticize government leaders or policy, and opposition access to radio and television time remained limited. Foreign media broadcast throughout the country, and cable news and other programming were available via satellite.

In 1992 the Ministry of Communication created a Communication Commission to distribute licenses to nongovernmental entities wishing to operate media outlets. In 2012 the ministry accepted its first application for licensing, but the application remained pending. In 2015 Maydaneh Abdallah Okieh--a journalist with radio station *La Voix de Djibouti*--submitted a request to the Ministry of Communication for approval to operate a radio station. He subsequently received a letter stating the ministry's commission had not been fully established and could not grant rights to operate a radio station. After the April cabinet reshuffle, the ministry selected members for the Communication Commission, but had yet to issue an official press release with all the names of members to formalize the commission.

<u>Violence and Harassment</u>: The government arrested and harassed journalists.

For example, on January 11, gendarmes arrested and detained *La Voix de Djibouti* journalist Mohamed Ibrahim Waiss for allegedly reporting on court cases of opposition members. He was in Gabode Prison on pretrial detention until January 17. Authorities dismissed his case on January 24 for lack of evidence.

<u>Censorship or Content Restrictions</u>: Media laws and the government's harassment and detention of journalists resulted in widespread self-censorship.

Circulation of a new newspaper requires authorization from the Communication Commission, which requires agreement from the National Security Service. The National Security Service reportedly investigated funding sources and the newspaper staff's political affiliations.

<u>Libel/Slander Laws</u>: The government used laws against slander to restrict public discussion.

In August, Youssouf Ahmed, editor of independent magazine *Le Renard*, was arrested and detained on charges of libel for criticizing high-level government officials. He was released after 48 hours. Authorities first sentenced Ahmed to one month in prison and a 9.96 million Djiboutian franc ($56,270) fine, but he settled his case out of court. According to opposition and human right groups, his case was dismissed contingent upon him no longer commenting on high-level government officials.

Internet Freedom

There were few government restrictions on access to the internet, although the government monitored social networks to ensure there were no planned demonstrations or overly critical views of the government (see section 1.c.).

Djibouti Telecom, the state-owned internet provider, reportedly continued to block access to websites of the Association for Respect for Human Rights in Djibouti and *La Voix de Djibouti*, which often criticized the government. According to the International Telecommunication Union, 10.71 percent of the population used the internet in 2015.

Academic Freedom and Cultural Events

There were government restrictions on academic and cultural events. Following the December 2015 incident, there was a presidential decree issued for security reasons that forbade any cultural, political, or religious gatherings for two months. The Ministry of Religious and Cultural Affairs postponed a regional folkloric dance and a regional conference of Muslim religious leaders due to the decree until after the presidential election in April.

Unlike in the previous year, there were no government restrictions on academic freedom.

b. Freedom of Peaceful Assembly and Association

Freedom of Assembly

Although the constitution provides for freedom of assembly, the government restricted this right. The Ministry of Interior requires permits for peaceful assemblies. In contrast with the previous year, the Ministry of Interior allowed opposition groups to host events and rallies, particularly for the presidential campaign. Security authorities occasionally restricted this right (see section 1.c.).

Freedom of Association

The constitution and law allow for freedom of association provided community groups register and obtain a permit from the Ministry of Interior. Nevertheless, the ministry ignored the petitions of some groups (see section 5). The government harassed and intimidated opposition parties, human rights groups, and labor unions.

c. Freedom of Religion

See the Department of State's *International Religious Freedom Report* at www.state.gov/religiousfreedomreport/.

d. Freedom of Movement, Internally Displaced Persons, Protection of Refugees, and Stateless Persons

The law generally provides for freedom of movement within the country, foreign travel, emigration, and repatriation, and the government generally respected these rights. The government collaborated with the Office of the UN High Commissioner for Refugees (UNHCR) to draft and pass a comprehensive refugee

law, ensuring refugees' right to health, education, and the right to work. The
National Assembly adopted the refugee law on December 26.

The government cooperated with UNHCR and other humanitarian organizations in
providing protection and assistance to refugees, asylum seekers, stateless persons,
and other persons of concern.

<u>Abuse of Migrants, Refugees, and Stateless Persons</u>: The government maintained
an increased police presence at the Ali Addeh refugee camp following the 2014
attack on La Chaumiere restaurant. Separately, gendarmes maintained a presence
at the Markazi refugee camp. Refugees had limited legal protections since there
were no permanent courts within the camps or in neighboring communities.

Refugees, however, reported abuse and attacks to the National Office for
Assistance to Refugees and Populations Affected by Disaster (ONARS) and
UNHCR. With the support of the local National Union of Djiboutian Women
(UNFD), mobile courts traveled to the largest camp, Ali Addeh, to hear the
backlog of pending cases. During the year UNFD also placed a full-time staff
member in all refugee camps to provide support for domestic violence victims.
Cases of domestic violence were reported, although the status of subsequent
investigations was unknown. Impunity remained a problem.

The government detained and deported large numbers of irregular migrants,
primarily from Ethiopia. The government sometimes gave individual irregular
migrants the opportunity to claim asylum status, after which the National
Eligibility Commission was supposed to determine their status. The commission
did not sit during the year until July 24. More than 8,042 asylum seekers awaited
decisions on their asylum claims.

<u>In-country Movement</u>: Due to the continuing border dispute with Eritrea, certain
areas in the north remained under military control.

<u>Foreign Travel</u>: Opposition members reported immigration officials prevented
them from boarding international flights.

For example, on August 9, gendarmes stopped Union for National Salvation (USN)
Secretary General Abdourahman Mohamed Guelleh at the entrance of the Ambouli
airport, preventing him from boarding his international flight. Government
officials stated Guelleh could not leave the country until his case concerning
alleged involvement in the December 2015 incident was closed. He remained

released on probation. On July 12, the Supreme Court dismissed Guelleh's case, but the state prosecutor overturned the decision. Guelleh's case remained pending.

Protection of Refugees

<u>Access to Asylum</u>: The law provides for the granting of asylum or refugee status. Asylum seekers from southern Somalia and Yemen are, prima facie, considered eligible for asylum or refugee status. All other asylum claims must be reviewed by the National Eligibility Commission, which falls under the Ministry of Interior and consists of staff from ONARS and several ministries; UNHCR participates as an observer.

According to UNHCR the country hosted more than 19,000 refugees and asylum seekers, primarily from south and central Somalia, Ethiopia, and Eritrea, in two refugee camps in the southern region of Ali Sabieh. An additional estimated 4,800 individuals from Ethiopia, Yemen, Somalia, and other nations lived in urban areas, primarily in Djibouti City. Due to Ethiopia's instability in August and September, the country permitted more than 5,000 Ethiopians, particularly those from the Oromia, to register as asylum seekers.

In the past most new Somali refugees arrived at the Ali Addeh camp, which reached maximum capacity several years previously. To reduce congestion, in 2012 UNHCR and ONARS reopened a second camp at Holl-Holl. UNHCR and ONARS completed a validation census of refugees in camps and in Djibouti City in January and identified those who arrived after 2009 for voluntary relocation to the new camp.

The country also hosted refugees fleeing violence in Yemen starting in March 2015. ONARS and UNHCR registered approximately 6,000 refugees from Yemen, at least 2,800 of whom lived in a refugee camp in the northern region of Obock.

Organizational difficulties and resource constraints prevented ONARS and UNHCR from providing adequate services to refugees in all camps and in Djibouti City, including the prompt processing of asylum claims.

Due to the unresolved conflict begun in 2008 between Djibouti and Eritrea and the mandatory military conscription policy of the Eritrean government, the government considered Eritrean detainees as deserters from the Eritrean military rather than refugees. Beginning in 2011, however, the government allowed

UNHCR to screen and resettle more than 200 Eritrean detainees imprisoned at Nagad in the United States, Canada, and Europe. In 2014 authorities released the 266 remaining Eritreans from Nagad and placed them in the Ali Addeh refugee camp. During the year the government continued to facilitate resettlement of this group. The government agreed to release 18 Eritrean detainees if the ICRC could resettle them to a third country. By year's end the ICRC had not found a third country for resettlement of the 18 detainees.

Refoulement: The government did not routinely grant refugee or asylum status to groups other than southern Somalis and--beginning in March 2015--Yemenis. A backlog in asylum status determinations put individuals waiting for their screening at risk of expulsion to countries where they might be threatened. In 2014 two suicide bombers from Somalia attacked La Chaumiere restaurant in Djibouti's city center, killing one victim and severely injuring others. Al-Shabaab claimed responsibility for this attack. After the attack, authorities closed the border with Somalia to refugees and stopped new registration and refugee status determination processes. Although the border remained officially closed during 2015, UNHCR reported the government allowed new arrivals into the country. The government also resumed the refugee status determination process in June 2015, hosting several sessions of the National Eligibility Commission each month thereafter.

Because of the presidential election and subsequent cabinet reshuffle, the National Eligibility Commission did not conduct interviews during the year until July 24. The Ministry of Interior-led commission met monthly from July to year's end to reduce the backlog.

Because of resource constraints and limited capacity, the government did not proactively screen irregular migrants to determine if they were trafficking victims before returning them to their home countries.

Most of these cases involved Ethiopian nationals, whom government officials often identified as economic migrants. The government, working with the International Organization for Migration (IOM), continued its efforts to differentiate refugees from irregular migrants. A lack of staff and other resources, however, impeded accurate vetting, particularly in light of the large number of irregular migrants transiting the country to Yemen and migrants deported from Yemen to Djibouti.

Employment: Scarce resources and employment opportunities limited local integration of refugees. Documented refugees were allowed to work with a work permit, and many (especially women) did so in jobs such as house cleaning, babysitting, or construction. There was little recourse to challenge working conditions or ensure fair payment for labor.

Access to Basic Services: The Ali Addeh camp was overcrowded, and basic services such as potable water were inadequate. The Holl-Holl camp was not overcrowded and had better access to potable water than the Ali Addeh camp. The government continued to issue birth certificates to children born in the Ali Addeh and Holl-Holl refugee camps. ONARS and UNHCR completed a refugee verification exercise in January 2015, which allowed ONARS and UNHCR officials to issue identification cards to all refugees older than 15 years in the Ali Addeh and Holl-Holl refugee camps and in Djibouti City. UNHCR and ONARS resumed resettlement activities in 2015, which had been on hold since 2012.

ONARS and UNHCR established the Markazi refugee camp in May 2015 after Yemenis began arriving in Djibouti following the eruption of violence in Yemen. The Markazi camp provided Yemeni refugees with basic services such as water, food, shelter, and medical services. The government issued birth certificates to children born in the Markazi refugee camp. ONARS and UNHCR also began issuing identification cards to Yemeni refugees.

For the first time, the government agreed to create a new Ministry of Education-recognized English curriculum for the 2017-18 academic year for more than 12,000 refugee children in the refugee camps. Previously UNHCR provided refugees in the Ali Addeh and Holl-Holl refugee camps with a Kenya-adapted curriculum taught in English and French that was not recognized by Kenyan and Djiboutian authorities.

Refugees in the Markazi camp had access to instruction based on a Yemeni and Saudi curriculum taught in Arabic.

Durable Solutions: In conjunction with IOM, the government continued to support vocational training for young refugees. These training programs have resulted in a small number of refugees finding local employment.

Temporary Protection: The government provided temporary protection to a limited number of individuals who may not qualify as refugees. Authorities often jailed irregular migrants identified as economic migrants attempting to transit the country to enter Yemen and returned them to their countries of origin. The government worked with IOM to provide adequate health services to these migrants while they awaited deportation. IOM and the Ministry of Health have a

Memorandum of Understanding permitting IOM to provide health supplies to hospitals in the "migration corridor" in Northern Djibouti, as well as enabling the ministry to have a health unit in IOM's Migration Resource Center in Obock.

Section 3. Freedom to Participate in the Political Process

The constitution and law provide citizens the ability to choose their government in free and fair periodic elections held by secret ballot and based on universal and equal suffrage. The government, however, deprived many citizens of this ability by suppressing the opposition and refusing to allow several opposition groups to form legally recognized political parties. The formal structures of representative government and electoral processes had little relevance to the real distribution and exercise of power.

Elections and Political Participation

Recent Elections: On April 19, the Constitutional Council proclaimed the official and final results of the April 8 presidential election and confirmed the reelection of President Ismail Omar Guelleh for a fourth term in the first round of voting. The Constitutional Council certified that Guelleh was reelected president with 111,389 of 127,933 votes cast, giving him 87.7 percent of the vote. Two opposition and three independent candidates shared the rest of the votes. One opposition group boycotted the election, stating the process was fraudulent. After the election opposition members noted irregularities, including alleging authorities unfairly ejected opposition delegates from polling stations, precluding them from observing the vote tallying. Most opposition leaders called the election results illegitimate.

International observers from the African Union, the Intergovernmental Authority on Development (IGAD), and the Arab League characterized the presidential election as "peaceful," "calm," and "sufficiently free and transparent," but noted irregularities. For example, international observers stated the Union for a Presidential Majority (UMP) coalition continued to provide campaign paraphernalia after the campaign period closed and on the day of the election. Some polling station workers also wore shirts and paraphernalia supporting the UMP. The African Union made a list of 13 recommendations, including the need for an independent electoral commission in charge of overseeing the election process and the counting of votes. The executive branch selected the members of the National Independent Electoral Commission (CENI).

In contrast to the presidential election, the 2013 legislative elections resulted in a narrow victory for the ruling UMP coalition. According to official results, the USN opposition coalition received 10 seats in the 65-member National Assembly. International observers from the African Union, IGAD, the Organization of Islamic Cooperation, and the Arab League characterized the election as free and fair, an assessment that domestic and international nongovernmental organizations (NGOs) criticized.

There was limited progress on implementing the 2014 framework agreement prior to the presidential election. Nevertheless, following the presidential election, National Assembly opposition leaders and UMP leaders resumed their discussions, as reflected in an October 20 open debate on government policies.

<u>Political Parties and Political Participation</u>: The government beat, harassed, and excluded some opposition leaders (see section 1.c.). The government also restricted the operations of opposition parties. According to Freedom House, opposition parties were also "disadvantaged by electoral rules and the government's abuse of the administrative apparatus."

For example, on March 28, one of the opposition presidential candidates organized a meeting for supporters in Dikhil and Ali Sabieh. According to human rights groups and opposition officials, security officials held the opposition presidential candidate and his group on the highway going from Djibouti to Dikhil for eight hours, preventing him from attending the rally. Gendarmes seized the phones of the presidential candidate and all other persons present. The gendarmes released the candidate after eight hours.

As in previous years, the Ministry of Interior refused to recognize three opposition political parties, although the political parties continued to operate: the Movement for Development and Liberty, the Movement for Democratic Renewal, and the Rally for Democratic Action and Ecological Development.

<u>Participation of Women and Minorities</u>: Women held eight of 65 seats in the National Assembly, and there were three women in the 23-member cabinet. The president of the Supreme Court, who by law acts as the country's president in case of the latter's death or incapacitation, was a woman. Custom and traditional societal discrimination resulted in a secondary role for women in public life.

For the presidential election, CENI had no female members. According to the African Union's observation mission, women represented 12 percent of personnel working at polling stations and on average 10 percent of delegates for each candidate.

Section 4. Corruption and Lack of Transparency in Government

The law provides criminal penalties for official corruption, but the government did not implement such laws effectively, and officials engaged in corrupt practices with impunity. According to the World Bank's most recent Worldwide Governance Indicators, government corruption was a serious problem. There were reports of government corruption.

Corruption: No known high-level civil servants were disciplined for corruption. The government ceased an initiative begun in 2012 to rotate accountants among government offices as a check on corruption. The law requires the court and the Inspectorate General to report annually, but both entities lacked resources, and reporting seldom occurred.

Financial Disclosure: Public officials were not subject to financial disclosure laws.

Public Access to Information: There were no laws providing for public access to government information, although legislative texts were publicly available through the online official journal, and citizens could address requests for information to the Ombudsman's Office.

Some government officials continued to block the publication of study results that might have reflected poorly on the government's performance, especially studies in which results could be compared with those of other countries.

Section 5. Governmental Attitude Regarding International and Nongovernmental Investigation of Alleged Violations of Human Rights

The government generally allowed a few domestic human rights groups that dealt with matters authorities did not consider politically sensitive to operate without restriction, conducting limited investigations and sometimes publishing findings on human rights cases. Government officials occasionally were responsive to their views. Government officials regularly cooperated with local associations offering training and education to citizens on human rights issues such as women's rights. Many of these associations had leaders who were also key officials of the government. Nevertheless, local human rights groups that covered politically sensitive matters did not operate freely and were often targets of government harassment and intimidation.

Following the death of human rights activist Jean Paul Noel Abdi in 2012, a group of civil servants from various ministries created the Djiboutian Observatory for the Promotion of Democracy and Human Rights. Although the organization applied for association status in 2012, 2013, 2014, and 2015, the Ministry of Interior had not granted the group formal status by year's end.

Government Human Rights Bodies: The government's National Human Rights Commission included technical experts, representatives of civil society and labor, religious groups, the legal community, the Ombudsman's Office, and the National Assembly. A 2014 law made the commission a permanent institution with increased staffing and regional offices. The commission last produced an annual report in 2013 and occasionally commented on cases of concern. State-run media featured prominent coverage of the commission's activities throughout the year, which included participation in human rights training workshops and visits by regional and international human rights representatives, such as the chairperson of the African Commission on Human and Peoples' Rights.

A government ombudsman holds responsibilities that include mediation between the government and citizens on issues such as land titles, issuance of national identity cards, and claims for unpaid wages. Written records of the ombudsman's activities were sparse, and it was unclear what actions he took during the year to promote human rights.

Section 6. Discrimination, Societal Abuses, and Trafficking in Persons

Women

Rape and Domestic Violence: The law includes sentences of up to 20 years' imprisonment for rape but does not address spousal rape. The government did not enforce the law effectively. Families of the victim and perpetrator usually settled rape cases using the traditional justice system. Women rarely reported rape cases to law enforcement officials, and reliable statistics were not available.

Domestic violence against women was common, but few cases were reported. While the law does not specifically prohibit domestic violence, it prohibits "torture and barbaric acts" against a spouse and specifies penalties up to 20 years' imprisonment for perpetrators. Rather than the courts, families and clans handled cases of violence against women. Police rarely intervened in domestic violence incidents, and the media reported only the most extreme cases, usually involving death of the victim.

The UNFD operated a walk-in counseling center (Cellule d'Ecoute) in Djibouti City that provided services and referrals for women and men. With the support of UNHCR, the UNFD also provided legal assistance to victims of sexual or gender-based violence in the refugee camps.

Female Genital Mutilation/Cutting (FGM/C): The law prohibits FGM/C, but it was a problem. According to a 2012 Ministry of Health survey, 78 percent of girls and women between the ages of 15 and 49 years had undergone FGM/C; in 2006 the figure was 93 percent. Infibulation, the most extreme form of FGM/C, with a prevalence of 67.2 percent, according to UNFD, continued, although with declining frequency. The law punishes perpetration of FGM/C by five years' imprisonment and a fine of one million Djibouti francs (DJF) ($5,650), and NGOs could file charges on behalf of victims. In late 2014 the government convicted two women for the first time on charges of committing FGM/C. Both women, one the excisor (cutter) and the other the mother of the victim, received six-month suspended sentences. This was reportedly the only conviction. The law also provides for up to one year's imprisonment and a fine of up to 100,000 DJF ($565) for anyone convicted of failing to report a completed or planned FGM/C to the proper authorities; however, the government had punished no one under this statute.

The government continued efforts to end FGM/C with a high-profile national publicity campaign, public support from the president's wife and other prominent women, and outreach to Muslim religious leaders. The media featured frequent and prominent coverage of events organized to educate the public on the negative consequences of FGM/C. According to government ministries, NGOs, and informal conversations with women, efforts by the UNFD and other groups to educate women were reportedly effective in lessening the incidence of FGM/C in the capital, changing perceptions of the practice, and empowering young girls themselves to say no to FGM/C. In collaboration with UNICEF, UNFD celebrated the Zero Tolerance Day for FGM/C in January, culminating in communities across the country and government officials declaring their support for ending FGM/C.

Sexual Harassment: The law does not prohibit sexual harassment, but anecdotal information suggested such harassment was widespread, although seldom reported.

According to UNFD, there were 168 documented cases of sexual harassment in 2015.

<u>Reproductive Rights</u>: Couples have the right to decide the number, spacing, and timing of their children; manage their reproductive health; and have access to the information and means to do so, free from discrimination, coercion, or violence. Clinics under the Ministry of Health operated freely in disseminating information on family planning. There were no restrictions on the right to access contraceptives, and a 2012 Ministry of Health survey estimated 22 percent of women of reproductive age used modern contraceptives. Misinformation about contraceptives, combined with a cultural preference for large families (between five and eight children), discouraged the use of contraceptives, especially in rural areas, where the coverage was only 12.9 percent.

The government provided childbirth services. Ninety-eight percent of childbirths in urban areas took place in health facilities, while 53 percent of childbirths in rural areas did, according to a 2012 Djibouti Family Health Survey study. The same study reported 88 percent of women received appropriate prenatal care. Although there was a large disparity between women in the capital and in rural areas, 53 percent of women received postpartum care. The UN Population Fund estimated the maternal mortality rate in 2015 at 292 deaths per 100,000 live births, down from 338 in 2001. The lack of facilities outside the capital and overall dearth of services contributed to poor maternal health outcomes.

<u>Discrimination</u>: The constitution provides for equal treatment of citizens without distinction concerning gender, but custom and traditional societal discrimination, including in education, resulted in a secondary role for women in public life and fewer employment opportunities in the formal sector. The law does not require equal pay for equal work (see section 7.d.). In accordance with sharia, men inherit a larger proportion of estates than do women. Many women owned and ran small businesses, although mostly in the informal sector, where they did not receive the same benefits or access to credit available in the formal sector. The government continued to promote female leadership in the small business sector, including through expanded access to microcredit.

A presidential decree requires that women hold at least 20 percent of all high-level public service positions, although the government has never implemented the decree. The Ministry for the Promotion of Women and Family Planning is responsible for promoting the rights of women and conducted awareness-raising events and workshops to combat discrimination.

Children

Birth Registration: Citizenship derives from a child's parents. The government continued to encourage the immediate registration of births, but confusion over the process sometimes resulted in children going without proper documentation. While most births in Djibouti City were ultimately registered, births in rural areas often were registered late or not at all. The birth registration fee of 2,000 DJF ($11.30) deterred some parents from registering births. Lack of birth registration did not result in denial of public services, but lack of such documentation prevented youth from completing their higher studies and adults from voting.

Education: Although primary education is compulsory, only an estimated 60 percent of children reportedly were enrolled in school. Primary and middle school are tuition free, but other expenses could be prohibitive for poor families. Although the educational system did not discriminate against girls, societal attitudes resulted in lower school enrollment rates for girls in some regions.

Child Abuse: Child abuse existed but was not frequently reported or prosecuted, and the government made only limited efforts to combat it.

Early and Forced Marriage: Although the law fixes the minimum legal age of marriage at 18 years, it provides that "marriage of minors who have not reached the legal age of majority is subject to the consent of their guardians." Child marriage occasionally occurred in rural areas, where it was considered a traditional practice rather than a problem. The Ministry for the Promotion of Women and Family Planning worked with women's groups throughout the country to protect the rights of girls, including the right to decide when and whom to marry.

Female Genital Mutilation/Cutting (FGM/C): See information for girls under 18 years old in women's subsection above.

Sexual Exploitation of Children: The law provides for three years' imprisonment and a fine of one million DJF ($5,650) for the commercial exploitation of children. The law does not specifically prohibit statutory rape, and there is no legal minimum age of consent. The sale, manufacture, or distribution of all pornography, including child pornography, is prohibited under laws prohibiting attacks on "good morals," and violations are punishable with a year in prison and a fine of up to 200,000 DJF ($1,130).

The government also passed and promulgated a new anti-trafficking-in-persons (TIP) law in March, which prohibits trafficking and outlines definitions distinguishing trafficking and smuggling. Contrary to the international definition of trafficking, the law requires the use of force, fraud, or coercion for a finding of child sex trafficking.

Despite government efforts to keep at-risk children off the streets and to warn businesses against permitting children to enter bars and clubs, children were vulnerable to prostitution on the streets and in brothels. Children were vulnerable to commercial sexual exploitation after reaching Djibouti City or the Ethiopia-Djibouti trucking corridor.

Displaced Children: More than 12, 078 children under the age of 18 years lived as registered refugees or asylum seekers in refugee camps or as urban refugees. Statistics on children living on the streets and on unaccompanied migrant children were unavailable, although NGOs reported an increasing number of unaccompanied minors living in Djibouti City or traveling through the country en route to the Middle East.

International Child Abductions: The country is not a party to the 1980 Hague Convention on the Civil Aspects of International Child Abduction. See the Department of State's *Annual Report on International Parental Child Abduction* at travel.state.gov/content/childabduction/en/legal/compliance.html.

Anti-Semitism

Observers estimated the Jewish community at fewer than 30 persons, the majority of whom were foreign military members stationed in the country. There were no reports of anti-Semitic acts.

Trafficking in Persons

See the Department of State's *Trafficking in Persons Report* at www.state.gov/j/tip/rls/tiprpt/.

Persons with Disabilities

The constitution does not prohibit discrimination against persons with disabilities, although the labor code prohibits discrimination in employment against such persons (see section 7.d.). Both the Ministry of National Solidarity and the

Ministry for the Promotion of Women and Family Planning had responsibility specifically to protect the rights of persons with disabilities. Nevertheless, due to resource constraints the law was not enforced. The government did not mandate access to government services and accessibility to buildings for persons with disabilities, and buildings were often inaccessible. The law provides persons with disabilities access to health care and education; however, the law was not enforced. The law does not prohibit discrimination against persons with disabilities in air travel and other transportation.

Authorities held prisoners with mental disabilities separately from other pretrial detainees and convicted prisoners. They received minimal psychological treatment or monitoring. Families could request to have relatives with mental disabilities who had not been convicted of any crime, but who were considered a danger to themselves or those around them, confined in prison. There were no mental health treatment facilities and only one practicing psychiatrist in the country.

Societal discrimination against persons with disabilities occurred. The National Human Rights Commission conducted awareness raising campaigns, and NGOs continued to organize seminars and other events that drew attention to the need for enhanced legal protections and better workplace conditions for persons with disabilities.

National/Racial/Ethnic Minorities

The governing coalition included all of the country's major clan and ethnic groups, with minority groups also represented in senior positions. Twelve ministers were of the Afar minority group. Nonetheless, there continued to be discrimination based on ethnicity in employment and job advancement (see section 7.d.). Somali Issas, the majority ethnic group, controlled the ruling party and dominated the civil service and security services. Discrimination based on ethnicity and clan affiliation remained a factor in business and politics.

Acts of Violence, Discrimination, and Other Abuses Based on Sexual Orientation and Gender Identity

The law does not directly criminalize consensual same-sex sexual conduct, but authorities prosecuted the public display of same-sex sexual conduct under laws prohibiting attacks on "good morals." No antidiscrimination law exists to protect LGBTI individuals. There were no reported incidents of societal violence or discrimination based on gender identity or sexual orientation, although this was likely due to victims being unwilling to report such abuse. Societal norms do not allow for the public discussion of homosexuality, and LGBTI persons generally did not openly acknowledge their sexual orientation or gender identity. There were no known LGBTI organizations.

HIV and AIDS Social Stigma

There were no reported cases of violence or discrimination against persons with HIV/AIDS, although stigma against individuals with the disease was widespread. Several local associations worked in collaboration with the government to combat social discrimination.

Section 7. Worker Rights

a. Freedom of Association and the Right to Collective Bargaining

The constitution and law provide for the right to form and join independent unions with prior authorization from the Ministry of Labor. The law provides the right to strike after providing advance notification. The labor code allows collective bargaining and fixes the basic conditions for adherence to collective agreements. The law prohibits antiunion discrimination and requires employers to reinstate workers fired for union activities. The Economic Free Zones (EFZs) operate under different rules, and the labor code does not apply in the EFZs.

These rights were restricted in several ways. The procedure for trade union registration, according to the International Labor Organization, is lengthy and complicated, allowing the Ministry of Labor virtually unchecked discretionary authority over registration. The government also requires unions to resubmit to this approval process following any changes to union leadership or union statutes, meaning each time there is a union election, the union must reregister with the government.

The law provides for the suspension of the employment contract when a worker holds trade union office. The law also prohibits membership in a trade union if an individual has prior convictions (whether or not the conviction is prejudicial to the integrity required to exercise union office). The law provides the president with broad discretionary power to prohibit or severely restrict the right of civil servants to strike, based on an extensive list of "essential services" that may exceed the limits of international standards.

The government neither enforced nor complied with applicable laws, including the law on antiunion discrimination. Resources provided to enforce the laws, including inspections, were inadequate. The Labor Inspectorate had insufficient resources to train inspectors, conduct regular preventive inspections, or pursue enforcement of previous cases. The most common remedy for violations was for the labor inspector to visit the offending business and explain how to correct the violation. If the business complied, there was no penalty. Available remedies and penalties for violations were insufficient to deter violations, particularly given the lack of enforcement.

The government also limited labor organizations' ability to register participants, thus compromising the ability of labor groups to operate. The government continued not to recognize the two independent labor unions or allow them to register as official labor unions. Two government-backed labor unions with the same names as the independent labor unions, sometimes known as "clones," serve as the primary collective bargaining mechanisms for many workers. Only members of government-approved labor unions attended international and regional labor meetings with the imprimatur of the government. Independent union leaders alleged the government suppressed independent representative unions by tacitly discouraging labor meetings.

Collective bargaining sometimes occurred and usually resulted in quick agreements. The National Council on Work, Employment, and Professional Training examined all collective bargaining agreements and played an advisory role in their negotiation and application. The council included representatives from labor, employers, and the government. Workers exercised the right to strike and occasionally disregarded the requirement for giving advance notification.

In disputes over wages or health and safety problems, the Ministry of Labor encouraged direct resolution by labor representatives chosen by the government and employers. Workers or employers could request formal administrative hearings before the Labor Inspectorate. According to the inspectorate, these hearings could last anywhere from one day for simple disputes to two or more months for complex cases.

There were no reports employers refused to bargain with unions or that employers avoided hiring workers with bargaining rights.

b. Prohibition of Forced or Compulsory Labor

In March the government passed and promulgated a new TIP law. The law prohibits all forms of forced or compulsory labor and strengthens tools available to prosecutors to convict and imprison traffickers. Prosecutors increasingly enforced the law, but law enforcement investigators had difficulties in identifying trafficking crimes. Nevertheless, law enforcement leadership sought out training for their respective investigative officers. On July 30, the Ministry of Justice led a roundtable for the World Day against Trafficking with representatives from relevant ministries, including law enforcement, and civil society. Citizens and migrants were vulnerable to conditions of forced labor, including as domestic servants in Djibouti City and along the Ethiopia-Djibouti trucking corridor. Parents or other adult relatives forced street children, including citizen children, to beg. Children also were vulnerable to forced labor as domestic servants and coerced to commit petty crimes, such as theft (see section 7.c.).

Also see the Department of State's *Trafficking in Persons Report* at www.state.gov/j/tip/rls/tiprpt/.

c. Prohibition of Child Labor and Minimum Age for Employment

The law prohibits all labor by, and employment of, children under 16 years of age. Government enforcement of child labor legislation was ineffective, however. The Ministry of Labor is responsible for monitoring workplaces and preventing child labor; however, a shortage of labor inspectors, vehicles, and other resources impeded investigations of child labor. Penalties were insufficient to deter violations. No inspections were conducted in response to possible violations of child labor laws.

Child labor, including the worst forms of child labor, existed throughout the country. Children were engaged in the sale of the narcotic khat, legal under local law. Family-owned businesses such as restaurants and small shops employed children at all hours. Children were involved in a range of activities such as shining shoes, washing and guarding cars, selling items, working as domestic servants, working in subsistence farming and with livestock, begging, and other activities in the informal sector. Children of both sexes worked as domestic servants.

Also see the Department of Labor's *Findings on the Worst Forms of Child Labor* at www.dol.gov/ilab/reports/child-labor/findings/.

d. Discrimination with Respect to Employment and Occupation

The law prohibits discrimination with respect to employment and occupation based on gender, age, race, color, social background, nationality or national ancestry, participation or nonparticipation in a trade union, or political and religious opinion. The Labor Inspectorate, however, lacked adequate resources to enforce the law effectively.

There is no law prohibiting discriminatory hiring practices based on disability, sexual orientation, gender identity, or HIV or other communicable disease status.

The government did not effectively enforce applicable law. According to disability advocates, there were not enough employment opportunities for persons with disabilities, and legal protections for such individuals were inadequate. The law does not require equal pay for equal work (see section 6).

By law foreign migrant workers who obtain residency and work permits enjoy the same legal protections and working conditions as citizens. These laws were not enforced, and migrant workers experienced discrimination.

e. Acceptable Conditions of Work

The national minimum wage was 35,000 DJF ($198) per month for public sector workers. The law does not mandate a minimum wage for the private sector, but provides that minimum wages be established by common agreement between employers and employees. According to the government statistics office, 79 percent of the population lived in relative poverty. The legal workweek is 48 hours over six days, a limit that applies to workers regardless of gender or nationality. The law mandates a weekly rest period of 24 consecutive hours and the provision of overtime pay at an increased rate fixed by agreement or collective bargaining. The labor code states overtime hours cannot exceed 60 hours per week and 12 hours per day. The law provides for paid holidays. The government sets occupational safety and health standards, which cover the country's main industries. The minimum wage, hours of work, and occupational safety and health standards were not effectively enforced, including in the informal economy.

There are no laws or regulations permitting workers to remove themselves from situations that endanger health or safety without jeopardizing continued employment.

There was a large informal sector, but no credible data on the number of workers employed there.

The Ministry of Labor is responsible for enforcing occupational health and safety standards, wages, and work hours; however, resources allotted to enforcement were insufficient, and enforcement was ineffective. The ministry employed one labor inspector and four controllers. The Labor Inspectorate conducted 30 inspections during the year based on complaints about illegal labor conditions and found labor law violations in every case. Because of lack of enforcement, penalties are insufficient to deter violations. Migrants were particularly vulnerable to labor violations. Workers across several industries or sectors sometimes faced hazardous working conditions, particularly in the construction sector and at the ports. According to the Labor Inspectorate, workers typically reported abuses only after being fired. In most cases, the claimed abuse was improper termination, not an abuse of safety standards. Data on workplace fatalities and accidents was not available.